This book
belongs to:

....

....

PUBLISHER'S NOTE

The dinosaurs in this book will look different from other books.

They are red, green, yellow, pink, and blue. This might feel strange

to you, but the truth is that no one knows what colors dinosaurs

were. So put away your preconceptions, turn the page, and step

back to a colorful prehistoric world . . .

Dr. Steve Brusatte • Daniel Chester

DAY OF THE
DINOSAURS

Step into a spectacular prehistoric world

WIDE EYED EDITIONS

Contents

Take a step back in time . . .

You're about to head off on an amazing journey. It's a trip through time, back into the world of the dinosaurs. After reading some facts about what dinosaurs were and when they lived, you'll start in the Triassic Period, when the first dinosaurs were running around in the shadows of their fierce crocodile cousins. Then you'll jump into the Jurassic Period, when dinosaurs grew to huge sizes and spread around the world. Your trip will end in the Cretaceous Period, when dinosaurs dominated the land and were at the peak of their success.

Be careful! This is not an easy journey. Danger lurks around every corner. Some of these dinosaurs are meat-eaters that can tear you apart with their teeth and claws. Others are smaller meat-eaters that work in teams to chase down their prey. Thankfully, many of the dinosaurs are gentle plant-eaters, although you don't want to make them upset because some of them are so huge that they could crush you with a single step. Always be alert, watch your back, and try to keep your distance from the dinosaurs. If you can remember these simple rules, this journey will be a marvelous trip into a lost world that existed millions of years in the past . . .

The age of the dinosaurs

TRIASSIC

252–201 million years ago

250 million
years ago

200 million
years ago

Plateosaurus

EARLY-MIDDLE
JURASSIC

201–163 million years ago

Huayangosaurus

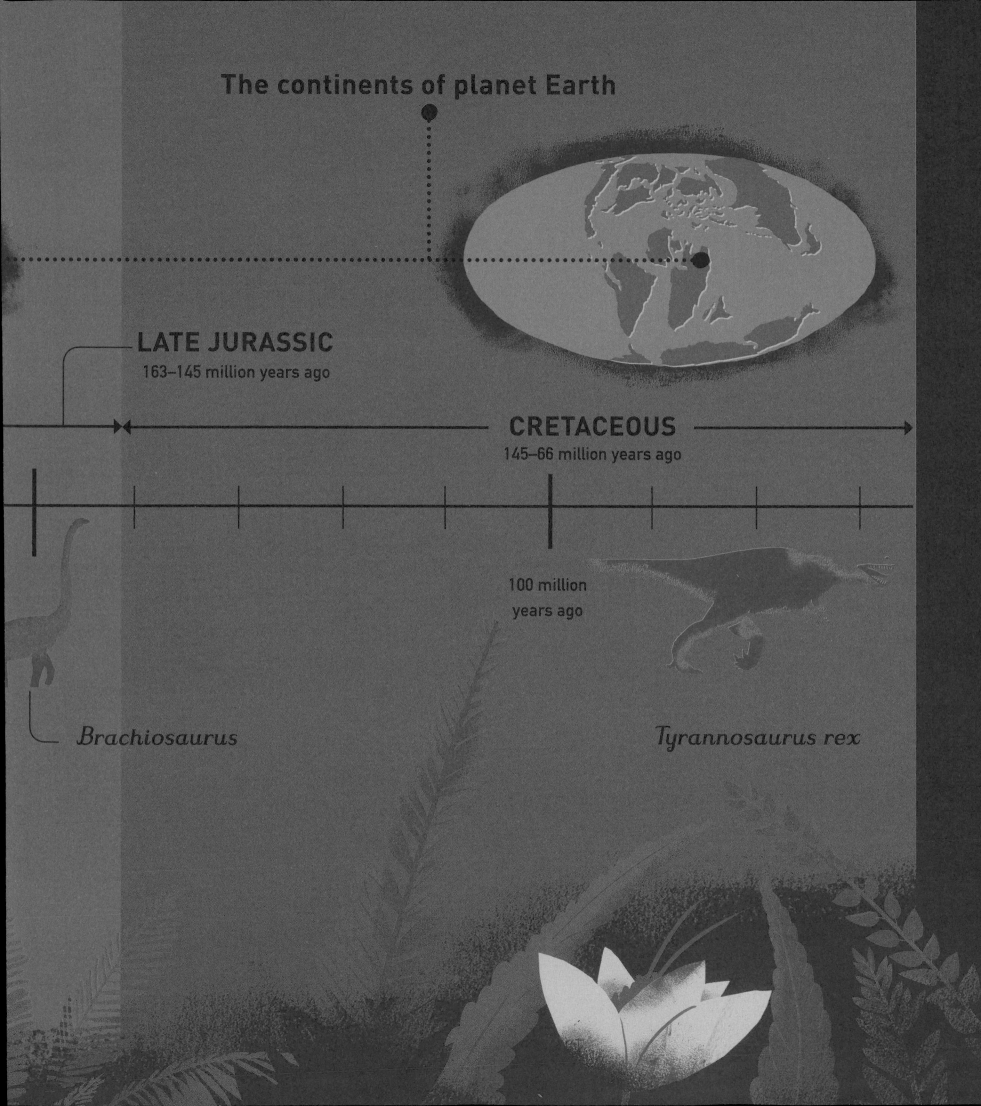

The continents of planet Earth

LATE JURASSIC
163–145 million years ago

CRETACEOUS
145–66 million years ago

100 million
years ago

Brachiosaurus

Tyrannosaurus rex

Who were the dinosaurs?

Dinosaurs first walked the earth about 230 million years ago. Though the word "dinosaur" means "terrible lizard" in Greek, dinosaurs weren't lizards, but a separate family of reptiles with common features like big muscles on the arms, and powerful jaws and legs held directly underneath the body, which allowed them to walk upright and move fast. Use this family tree as a reference when you're on your journey through the prehistoric world.

DROMAEOSAURS
Velociraptor
Agile predators with clawed hands and a killing claw on the hind foot.

BIRDS
Archaeopteryx
The only dinosaurs that exist today are small, feathered, and can fly!

TYRANNOSAURS
Tyrannosaurus rex
With powerful teeth and jaws, these are the killing machines of the Cretaceous!

CERATOSAURS
Ceratosaurus
Medium-sized, wiggly-tailed meat-eaters of the Jurassic.

PROSAUROPODS
Plateosaurus
Early plant-eaters related to the sauropods, but smaller.

COELOPHYSOIDS
Coelophysis
Small, fast-running predators of the Triassic and Early Jurassic.

SAUROPODS
Diplodocus
Long-necked herbivores weighing up to 60 tons!

SAUROPODOMORPHA

THEROPODA

LIZARD-HIPPED DINOSAURS
Saurischian means "lizard-hipped." Like lizards, the hip bones of saurischian dinosaurs point forward and down. All meat-eaters were lizard-hipped, but some plant-eaters were, too.

SAURISCHIANS

PACHYCEPHALOSAURS

Pachycephalosaurus
"Bonehead" dinosaurs with thick skulls, found in the Cretaceous.

SEA CREATURES

Dinosaurs weren't the only reptiles around in the prehistoric age. In the sea, long-necked plesiosaurs and dolphin-like ichthyosaurs roamed the waves.

PTEROSAURS

Dinosaurs, apart from birds, lived on land and weren't able to fly. However, pterosaurs could. These ancient winged reptiles were cousins of the dinosaurs.

CERATOPSIANS

Triceratops
Horned plant-eaters of the Cretaceous period.

ORNITHOPODS

Parasaurolophus
Fast-running herbivores with grinding teeth.

STEGOSAURS

Stegosaurus
Plated plant-eaters of the Jurassic and Early Cretaceous.

ANKYLOSAURS

Ankylosaurus
Armored dinosaurs with spikes, common in the Cretaceous.

MARGINOCEPHALIA

THYREOPHORA

ORNITHISCHIANS

BIRD-HIPPED DINOSAURS

Ornithischian means "bird-hipped." All ornithischian dinosaurs were herbivores. Their hip bones pointed backward, giving more room for big digestive organs that were needed to process plants.

WELCOME TO THE
TRIASSIC

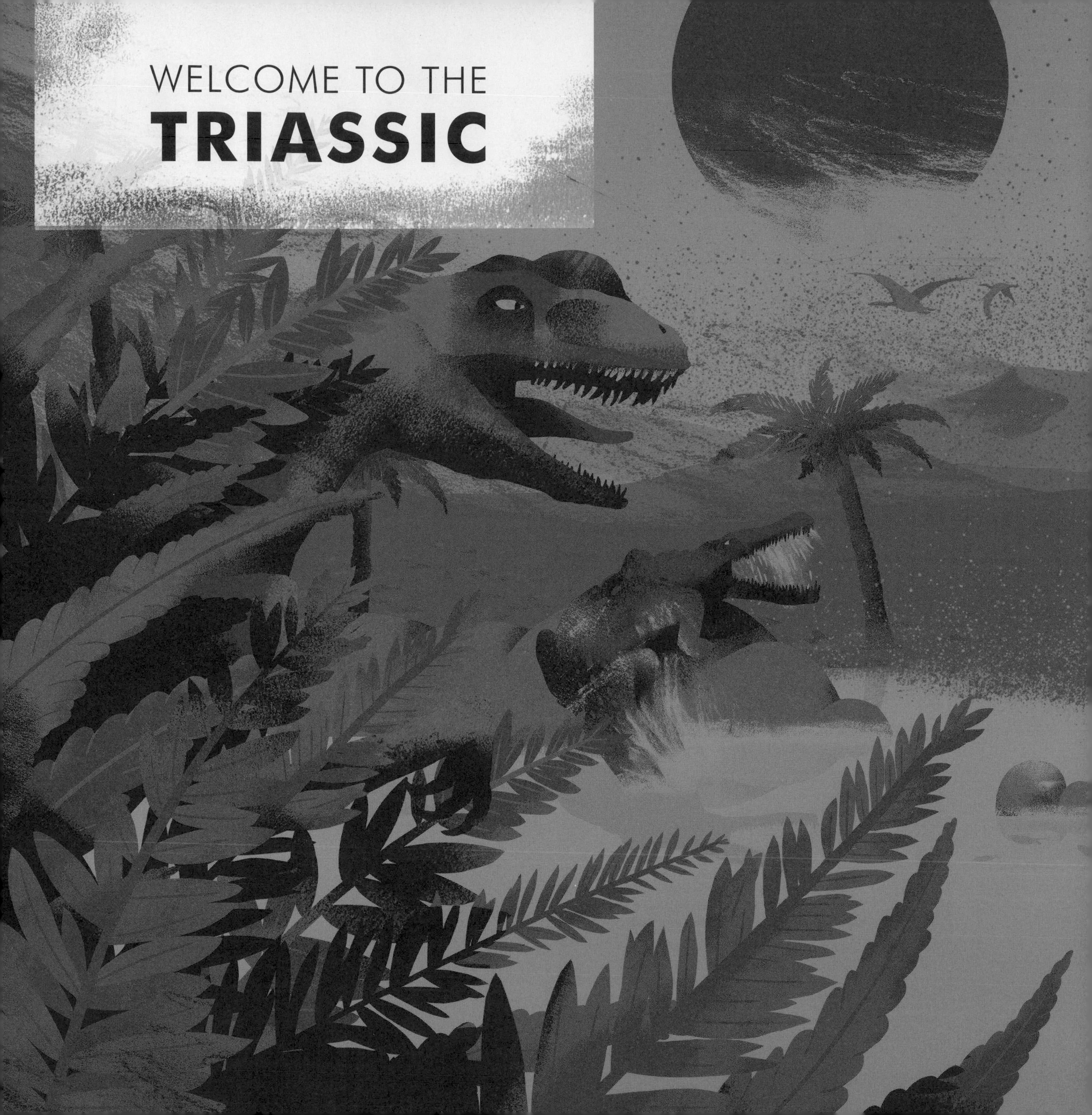

It's 210 million years ago. In the middle of a desert, a herd of plant-eating *Plateosaurus* gather around a lake to cool themselves from the hot sun. The temperature is over 104 degrees Fahrenheit and they have been walking for miles across sand dunes that burn their feet. Like you, they desperately need a drink . . . but the lake isn't a safe place. A giant salamander with hundreds of sharp teeth lurks in the water. An even larger meat-eating phytosaur waits patiently along the shore, hoping the *Plateosaurus* will come closer for a drink and—SNAP! Dinnertime. But then out of the fern grove races another predator, the dinosaur *Liliensternus*. As it closes in on the *Plateosaurus* herd, the phytosaur wonders if any food will be left for him. You back away from the attack, thinking you'll have to find water elsewhere.

Welcome to the Triassic . . .

Life in the desert

As you travel through the Triassic landscape, you notice it's dry and sandy. But then you find an oasis—a place in the desert with thick forests of ferns and evergreen trees. These plants are delicious food for many types of animals, and soon you spot some of the first long-necked dinosaurs! Some of the other plant-eating animals you see are early cousins of mammals, or strange reptiles that didn't survive past the Triassic.

The neck of *Plateosaurus* is longer than most Triassic dinosaurs, allowing it to feed higher in the trees. Descendants of *Plateosaurus* are the huge long-necked sauropods like *Brontosaurus* and *Diplodocus*.

Plateosaurus: This dinosaur is a plant-eating machine. The very biggest adults are 33 feet long and weigh 4 and a half tons.

Aetosaurus: It's one of the strangest sights in the Triassic: a herd of small, slow-moving, plant-eating *Aetosaurus*. This reptile has a long, skinny body and short arms.

Four rows of thick bony plates cover its body, providing great protection from predators like *Herrerasaurus*.

Hyperodapedon: *Hyperodapedon* is one of the weirdest animals you see in the Triassic. It's a rhynchosaur, a type of reptile related to dinosaurs. Its body is green and scaly, and it moves slowly, like a crocodile or a lizard.

It uses its strange-looking snout, which has a beak at the front and rows of teeth along the sides, to cut plants like a giant pair of scissors.

Placerias: This pot-bellied plant-eater is an early relative of mammals—like a prehistoric cow. It's big and fat and slow. Adults can grow over 11 feet long and weigh over a ton.

You see *Placerias* traveling in herds, searching for plants to slice with their beak and cut with their teeth.

14

SCALE

Antetonitrus is a close cousin of *Plateosaurus*, but is even bigger.

It is a classic sauropod dinosaur: it has a small head, long neck, huge belly, and arms and legs that are as thick as tree trunks to support its heavy body.

Antetonitrus walks on four legs and moves very slowly. You see it standing around all day, neck reaching high into the trees, eating and eating and eating.

Pisanosaurus: The puny plant-eating dinosaur *Pisanosaurus* is only 3 feet long, but it can run away quickly on its two legs if a predator approaches.

It's hard for you to spot because it blends in easily among the shrubs of the forest floor, where it munches on delicious ferns.

15

Prehistoric killers

You nervously look over your shoulder as you move through the trees. The Triassic is a terrifying time. Predators of all shapes and sizes wait in the shadows, hungry for their next meal. Some of these meat-eaters are early dinosaurs, but others are giant salamanders, or close cousins of crocodiles. Just when you think you've escaped, another beast jumps out and the chase is on . . .

Postosuchus: You see something huge and your heart stops. It's the Triassic animal you should fear the most: the terrifying *Postosuchus*.

Eodromaeus: This dinosaur doesn't look very scary to you ... It's only about the size of a small poodle. But this feisty meat-eater can run fast, hide easily and has sharp teeth, and claws to catch prey.

Eodromaeus is an early type of theropod dinosaur, a group of carnivores that run on strong hind legs. It is the great-great-grandfather of *Tyrannosaurus rex* and *Velociraptor*.

Postosuchus is over 16 feet long, weighs 660 pounds and has huge jaws that crush prey. It moves quickly on its long legs, fast enough to outrun almost any dinosaur. And if anyone tries to fight back, it's covered with bony plates that protect its body.

SCALE

Smilosuchus: At the edge of a lake, you catch a glimpse of *Smilosuchus* and think you're looking at a giant, angry crocodile. In fact, it's a phytosaur: a type of ferocious predator closely related to crocodiles and alligators.

It measures nearly 20 feet with a head about as long as a human is tall, full of cone-shaped teeth that can easily pierce flesh. Time to run...fast.

Tawa: The Triassic is a desert world, but there are some parts of the planet that get a lot of rain. Here's where you spot the king of these wetter environments: *Tawa*, a smart and fast-running predator that is closely related to *Eodromaeus*, but bigger.

Marasuchus: You blink and almost miss this little insect eater. Its tiny body is only the size of a cat, so it can easily hide from predators.

If a phytosaur or a dinosaur tries to catch it, *Marasuchus* can hop away on its long, muscular legs like a rabbit, or run away as fast as a cheetah.

Tawa travel in big herds of adults, each nearly 10 feet long from head to tail, working together to chase down their prey.

Herrerasaurus: Most Triassic dinosaurs are small, like *Eodromaeus*. But *Herrerasaurus* is a different kind of beast. It's about the size of a horse, but from your hiding place you see you don't want to ride this animal!

Herrerasaurus is a top predator, using its muscular arms and enormous claws to hunt. Like *Eodromaeus*, *Herrerasaurus* is an early theropod dinosaur, but it is much more frightening than its tiny cousin.

Metoposaurus: You know to stay far away from rivers and lakes, because *Metoposaurus* is waiting, ready to eat anything that walks too close to the shore.

The big, flat head has hundreds of little teeth, even on the roof of its mouth. *Metoposaurus* even hunts dinosaurs and *Postosuchus* from time to time.

It is a close relative of salamanders, but it differs from them in one major way: it's huge! At 8 feet long, *Metoposaurus* is the size of a small car.

Deep blue sea

It's hot and you're desperate for a swim, so you head to the beach. One vast ocean, called Panthalassa, covers the globe during the Triassic. It surrounds the single piece of land—known as a supercontinent—of Pangea. As well as fish, many different types of sea-living, air-breathing reptiles thrive in its cool blue waters. Some eat nothing but clams and oysters, some are bigger fish-eaters, and some are monstrous predators at the top of the food chain. As you walk into the waves, you know you've got to watch out . . .

Pachypleurosaurus: The fast, sleek, 3-foot long *Pachypleurosaurus* darts around you in the water, sneaking up on fish and then devouring them whole.

Pachypleurosaurus can swim so fast because it has a long, skinny skeleton just like an eel. It also has large hands and feet that act as paddles, helping it to move through the water even faster.

Nothosaurus: A bigger version of *Pachypleurosaurus* glides by. Much bigger. At 13 feet long *Nothosaurus* is a top predator, using a skull full of needle-shaped teeth to catch fish. It can't swim as fast as its smaller cousin, but still sneaks up on its prey. Sometimes, when there aren't enough fish to eat, *Nothosaurus* uses its flippers to dig into the bottom of the ocean and bring up worms and other creatures living in the mud.

SCALE

Shonisaurus: You're really hoping you don't see this animal. One of the biggest creatures in the Triassic ocean, 50-foot *Shonisaurus* is the king of the sea.

Shonisaurus is a type of ichthyosaur, a reptile that looks like a dolphin or a big fish, with a long, skinny snout full of sharp teeth, flippers for limbs, and a big tail just like a whale.

It travels in packs, so if you see one, others probably aren't far away ...

Cartorhynchus: You catch a glimpse of something in the distance that looks like a cross between a snake and a seal. It has a long snakelike body, stretching over 3 feet in length, and swims fast by wiggling this body back and forth.

It has a small head and sucks up soft prey, such as squids and small fish, like a powerful vacuum cleaner. Its flippers help with swimming, but also allow *Cartorhynchus* to flop around on land, like a seal on the beach.

Pistosaurus: The water moves in front of you, and you hear a rumbling sound in the distance. It must be *Pistosaurus*! This sea-living reptile has a big belly, a long neck, and huge flippers. It eats fish, using an array of sharp teeth to grab its slippery prey.

Catching prey can be tricky because *Pistosaurus* is no speed demon. It can't move its body very easily, because its stomach is so big, so it uses its flippers to move itself along.

Placodus: This eats nothing but oysters, clams, and other small animals with shells. It has big teeth at the front of its snout that it uses to snap up shellfish from the ocean bottom, like one of those giant claws in a carnival game. Then it uses its remaining teeth—which are big, flat plates that smash together—to crush the shells.

Fliers and tree jumpers

There are no birds around in the Triassic. They will come later, during the Jurassic. But as you look up, you see the skies are not empty. Flapping and soaring in the breeze are many species of pterosaurs, winged reptiles that are close cousins of dinosaurs. Many other types of strange reptiles live high in the trees, jumping and gliding between the branches.

Eudimorphodon: Flocks of *Eudimorphodon* gather in the sky, deciding what they should eat. Should they attack a swarm of insects over to their left? Or should they dive 300 feet below, into the water, and feast on some fish?

Eudimorphodon can choose what it eats because it has many different types of teeth. Some can be used to slice flesh, others to crush insects.

Megalancosaurus: If you want a Triassic pet, you should choose *Megalancosaurus*. It's small, only about a foot long, and has cute big eyes and colorful skin. It uses its tail to grab on to branches, and its feet have long, curving fingers to hold on tight.

This little reptile can't fly, but it lives high above the ground in the trees, far out of reach of the hungry dinosaurs down below.

SCALE

Austriadactylus: You look up to see something flying fast, maneuvring in the air like a fighter plane. *Austriadactylus* is a close cousin of *Eudimorphodon.*

Like all pterosaurs, *Austriadactylus* has a light body and a very long finger (like our ring finger) on its hands. A thin but strong sheet of skin stretches backward from this finger, making up the wing. *Austriadactylus* has a wingspan of about 3 feet.

Sharovipteryx: High in the trees there is a rustling sound. You can just make out a tiny animal, a bit like a fruit bat with a big sheet of skin on its body sticking out to the sides.

The wing you see is not on the arms, or supported by ribs, like *Kuehneosaurus*. Instead, the wing is on the legs! Say hello to *Sharovipteryx*, a strange reptile that glides between the trees.

Kuehneosaurus: This reptile is about the size of an iguana. It has wings, but they are not on the arms, like the wings of birds or pterosaurs. Instead, they are supported by long ribs that stick out of the body!

Mecistotrachelos: This small, rat-sized reptile looks like *Kuehneosaurus*. It also has big wings sticking out from its body, anchored by ribs. These wings are huge for its size.

Mecistotrachelos are very rare animals, and like to keep a low profile to avoid predators, so you'll be lucky to see one.

Kuehneosaurus cannot flap its ribs, so it can't really fly. Instead, it uses its wings as a parachute, to break its fall when it is jumping between trees.

You've seen Triassic dinosaurs eating all types of food. Some, like *Herrerasaurus* and *Tawa*, eat meat, others, like *Pisanosaurus* and *Antetonitrus*, eat plants. And some, like *Plateosaurus*, eat meat when it's available, but also munch plants, insects, nuts, and roots. How can dinosaurs eat so many different things? Here is your guide to the different types of skulls and teeth of dinosaurs, all adapted to eat particular types of food.

Sharp teeth

It is usually easy to tell if a dinosaur is a meat-eater. Just work up the courage to look into its mouth. Carnivores like *Tawa* have sharp, curved teeth, which are the perfect shape for hooking into flesh. These teeth also have tiny sharp points called serrations, like you get on a saw blade or a knife. They are perfect for slicing into prey.

Huge head

Like most predators, the head of *Herrerasaurus* is big compared to its body. Why? First, it needs big, powerful jaws to snatch its prey, and second, it needs a head big enough to handle the force of these jaws crunching through bone and flesh. Herbivores have smaller heads compared to their body as they don't need this biting power.

Mighty jaws

The head of *Postosuchus*, a relative of crocodiles, is also massive. In fact, this reptile walks on all fours because it doesn't need to use its arms to grab its dinner. Its jaws are so deep and powerful that they're all *Postosuchus* needs to snatch prey. Sharp daggerlike teeth rip apart anything it attacks.

Leaf teeth

Pisanosaurus is a plant-eater. Its teeth are very different from those of meat-eaters. They are not thin, sharp, and curved, and do not have fine serrations for cutting flesh. Instead, they are thicker, flatter, and shaped more like a leaf. This shape is perfect for snipping plants off a branch and then grinding them in the mouth.

Meat and veg

Plateosaurus is something of a cross between a plant-eating and a meat-eating dinosaur. Most of the time it eats plants, and has leaf-shaped teeth similar to *Pisanosaurus* that it uses to grind leaves, stems, and branches. But sometimes it eats insects and small animals like lizards and frogs, which it grabs with the sharper cone-shaped teeth at the front of its mouth.

Stomach stones

Many long-necked dinosaurs such as *Antetonitrus* have got stones in their big bellies. These are known as gastroliths. Sauropods tend to swallow leaves without chewing them very well, so these gastroliths move about, helping grind the plants up so they're easier for the dinosaurs to digest.

As you know, it's a dangerous world on the Triassic supercontinent of Pangea. In order to survive, the predators evolve sharp teeth and claws so they can hunt for food. The prey then evolve tools like armor plates to protect themselves, and then the predators evolve even more deadly weapons to defeat the prey. This arms race goes on and on and on . . . Use these notes to understand the ways the dinosaurs in the Triassic defend and attack.

Grabbing hands

Herrerasaurus is one of the top predators of the Triassic. It has sharp teeth to cut up prey, but those are not its only weapons. It also has muscular arms, which end in enormous hands with huge claws on the inner three fingers. These are perfect tools for grabbing its victims.

What big eyes you have . . .

Coelophysis will probably see you before you see it. The large eyes are bigger than normal for a creature of its size, helping the meat-eater spot prey hidden in bushes and undergrowth. If that's not enough, it hunts in packs, meaning an animal under attack doesn't just have to avoid one keen pair of eyes, but many.

Hide and seek

Marasuchus is a meat-eater, but it's no match for a hungry *Postosuchus* or even *Coelophysis*. It's tiny! But being the size of a cat is very helpful when you're trying to avoid the terrifying predators of the Triassic. It's able to hide behind plants and rocks to avoid becoming someone's dinner. Also, being so small means it may get overlooked if larger prey is available.

Claw slash

How is a peaceful plant-eating dinosaur supposed to defend itself from the vicious attacks of a carnivore like *Tawa* or *Herrerasaurus*? Some dinosaurs, like *Plateosaurus*, have a big, sharp claw on their thumb. They use this claw to slash at predators who try to eat them. If there are no predators around, the clawed hands are useful for pulling down branches and leaves to eat.

Too big to attack

Not all plant-eaters have sharp thumb claws that they can swing at predators. *Antetonitrus* is one of these dinosaurs. It walks on four legs, so it cannot swipe a predator with its hands. So what can *Antetonitrus* do? The answer is: nothing. It is so big that it uses its large size as a weapon. It can just stand there while small meat-eating dinosaurs try to bite and claw at its thick skin.

Bony armor

Some reptiles aren't big like *Antetonitrus*, but have evolved to protect themselves in a different way. *Aetosaurus* has four rows of thick bony plates covering its tanklike body. These plates are so strong that even the sharp teeth of predators like *Herrerasaurus* can't get through them to the flesh below.

Dinosaur features: *Herrerasaurus*

What does it mean to be a dinosaur? Many of the animals you've seen in the Triassic are dinosaurs: like *Herrerasaurus*, *Tawa*, *Plateosaurus*, *Antetonitrus*, and *Pisanosaurus*. But many others are not. Pterosaurs like *Eudimorphodon*, phytosaurs like *Smilosuchus*, and sea reptiles like *Pistosaurus* are not dinosaurs, though they are related. How do scientists know this? Because all dinosaurs share certain features. These features are only seen in dinosaurs, not in other types of animals like lizards or mammals.

Tail
The tail of *Herrerasaurus* is very long, about as long as the rest of the body. Why is this? Because the tail is used for balance. The body of *Herrerasaurus* is a lot like a seesaw, with the long tail making sure that the heavy front of the body (with the big head and stomach) does not fall over.

This long tail makes it easier for *Herrerasaurus* to move fast. Even dinosaurs that walk on four legs have long tails, which they use to defend themselves from predators.

WALK LIKE A DINOSAUR

Dinosaurs walk straight upright, with their legs directly beneath their body. Close relatives of dinosaurs like crocodiles and lizards walk very differently. Their legs sprawl out sideways from their bodies. Animals with legs directly underneath, like dinosaurs, are able to move much more smoothly than animals that sprawl.

Big muscles
All dinosaurs have big muscles on the arms, shoulders, and chest. For dinosaurs like *Herrerasaurus*, these muscles help them to grab and slash prey. For others, like *Antetonitrus*, these muscles are used in walking.

Jaw
The jaw muscles of dinosaurs are huge. They attach to the bones at the back of the skull, and are covered by skin.

Bite
The muscles that close the jaw are especially massive. They allow dinosaurs to bite very strongly.

Long legs
Herrerasaurus has long legs, which also help it run very fast. This is true of all dinosaurs. But not all dinosaurs walk the same. Many, like *Herrerasaurus*, walk only on their legs, while others, like *Antetonitrus*, walk on both their arms and legs. Most dinosaurs can move much faster than lizards and crocodiles.

LIFE CYCLE

Dinosaurs grow fast. All dinosaurs hatch from eggs, and grow from a hatchling to a teenager in just a few years. Some of the largest dinosaurs, like *Tyrannosaurus rex*, become adults around age twenty and don't live for more than thirty years. Crocodiles and lizards grow much, much slower.

WELCOME TO THE EARLY-MIDDLE
JURASSIC

It's 170 million years ago. You look out across a shallow lagoon, feeling the rain run down your face. Through the fog you see something big coming into view, stomping through the water. You get ready to run ... But it's only *Cetiosaurus*, a gentle giant with a long neck and tiny head who's come to eat the trees and bushes that grow along the seashore. Then, as you glance around, you notice something a lot scarier: two sharp-toothed meat-eaters, their eyes focused on the big sauropod. They're working together to stalk their prey.

Welcome to the Early-Middle Jurassic ...

Movers and shakers

As you walk through the Early-Middle Jurassic, you notice something. The dry desert has given way to floodlands and rainforest, and there are a lot more dinosaurs around. We're not exactly sure why, but at the end of the Triassic Period, many reptiles went extinct. This meant that dinosaurs had most of the world to themselves. Many new groups of plant-eaters evolved in the Early-Middle Jurassic, including armored dinosaurs like the plate-backed stegosaurs and tanklike ankylosaurs. Others, like the long-necked sauropods, started to grow to earth-shaking sizes.

Huayangosaurus: *Huayangosaurus* has big plates of bone, shaped like triangles, sticking out of its back. These flat, thin plates are covered in something slightly shiny, like your fingernails. In fact, this is the same material: keratin. It protects the plates and can also change colors to help *Huayangosaurus* camouflage itself, to hide from predators!

Heterodontosaurus: *A* funny little dinosaur, about the size of a dog, runs up to you. It is fluffy, covered with what look like long hairs all over its body. You reach down to pet it, but the pint-sized plant-eater growls, and you can see two sharp cone-shaped teeth in its lower jaw. These tusks are used to fight rivals over food or territory. Time to back away...

Scelidosaurus: This plant-eater is fairly big, about 13 feet long. It walks slowly on all four legs.

As you look closer, you see something you've never seen before. There are thick little circles of bone covering most of *Scelidosaurus*' body. They are arranged in rows that extend down the back and neck. It uses this armor to protect itself from meat-eating dinosaurs.

Shunosaurus: The long-necked *Shunosaurus* is usually a gentle animal. It spends most of its days sticking its big neck high into the trees and guzzling down mouthful after mouthful of leaves and stems.

If it's threatened, *Shunosaurus* has a big spiky club at the end of its tail that it uses to protect itself from its enemies. So don't get too close!

SCALE

Sarahsaurus: You take one look at the hands of *Sarahsaurus* and jump back into the trees. All of the fingers have claws, and the claw on the thumb is bigger than your hand! But you need not be scared. *Sarahsaurus* is a plant-eater. It uses these claws to grab on to trees and pull down branches, and occasionally to protect itself from the meat-eaters.

Vulcanodon: You hear *Vulcanodon* long before you can see it. This big long-necked sauropod makes a mighty noise with each step. You would too if you were over 20 feet long and weighed 11 tons!

Though *Vulcanodon* is huge, it is a peaceful creature that eats plants like big pine trees all day. It will leave you alone if you leave it alone.

On the hunt

You thought the Triassic was frightening, but the predators of the Early-Middle Jurassic will give you nightmares. With all those new plant-eating dinosaurs to feed on, the meat-eaters have got bigger, scarier, and hungrier. These dinosaurs roam the earth on the hunt for their next meal. As you continue on your journey, be sure to watch your back . . .

Proceratosaurus: This little guy doesn't look very scary. It seems kind of cute, although at over 6 feet long, it's a little too big to make a good pet. But don't be fooled. *Proceratosaurus* is smart, fast, and mean. It gobbles up little lizards and mammals in bunches.

Dilophosaurus: *As you're hiking in the sand dunes you hear a terrible scream in the distance. It sounds like something is hurt. You race up the closest dune, get out your binoculars, and look off to your left. What you see is terrifying: the meat-eater Dilophosaurus about to rip the flesh off a small long-necked dinosaur called Sarahsaurus.*

Dilophosaurus is a 22-foot-long meat-eater. Like many theropods of this time, it has a funny head crest. But it's not a good idea to laugh.

SCALE

Kileskus: *T. rex* is the most famous dinosaur of all, a 40-foot, 8-ton killing machine that bites through the bones of its prey. But where did *T. rex* come from? That would be *Kileskus*, the very oldest member of the tyrannosaur family and the ancestor of the great rex.

Kileskus is not a giant like its cousin, *T. rex*. It is only a little bigger than a human. But it definitely has a taste for meat.

Eoabelisaurus: *Eoabelisaurus* is the ancestor of the fearsome *Carnotaurus* and *Majungasaurus*, dinosaurs that were almost the size of *T. rex*, and terrorized much of the world during the Cretaceous period.

Megalosaurus: A loud roar echoes out from the forest. Stay back, because *Megalosaurus* is lurking in the bushes, waiting to jump out and snatch its next snack.

Megalosaurus is the king of the Middle Jurassic and at the top of the food chain. It's 23 feet long from snout to tail, weighs a ton and a half, and boasts a big head full of razor-sharp teeth. Not many dinosaurs can hunt down the long-necked sauropods, but *Megalosaurus* has the right tool kit.

Like other theropod meat-eaters, *Eobelisaurus* has a lightweight body and long, strong legs like a sprinter, letting it reach speeds of up to 25 miles per hour. As you stare up at one, its nostrils flaring, you know you better run...and fast!

Monolophosaurus: These Jurassic theropods just keep getting stranger. Up next is *Monolophosaurus*. It looks like it has a Mohawk haircut. You get out a pair of binoculars and look from a safe distance. It isn't hair, but a crest: a single big fan of bone sticking out from the top of its head.

Cryolophosaurus: *Cryolophosaurus* is a close cousin of *Dilophosaurus*, and about the same size. It also has a strange bit of bone sticking out of its head. This bony crest kind of looks like the flopped-over hairdo of Elvis Presley. But don't laugh, because *Cryolophosaurus* can hunt you down and use its sharp claws and teeth to eat you for dinner.

The head crest of *Cryolophosaurus*, like the other crests of theropods in this period, is used to attract female mates or intimidate rivals.

Underneath *Monolophosaurus*'s crest, there is a mouth filled with many knifelike teeth lining the jaws, perfect for biting into prey.

Watery worlds

As you exit the forest you're surprised to come across another beach. In the Triassic there was one ocean surrounding one huge bit of land. But in the Early-Middle Jurassic, this supercontinent is beginning to break up into many smaller pieces. As this happens, new oceans are slowly filling the gaps between the new smaller continents. And living in these oceans are many reptiles that spend all of their time in the water. Some are innocent little fish-eaters, but others are monstrous predators that must be avoided at all costs.

Ichthyosaurus: You stick your head underwater during a swim and get the shock of your life. Something that looks like a dolphin is about to get eaten by a terrifying predator …

This unlucky reptile is about 6 and a half feet long, has a fin on its back like a shark, and flippers for arms and feet. It's *Ichthyosaurus*, a member of a group of dolphin-like reptiles called ichthyosaurs that eat fish and squid, and were preyed on by *Liopleurodon*.

Liopleurodon: Everything in the ocean fears one beast above the rest: *Liopleurodon*. This monster is at the top of the food chain and eats whatever it wants, which is usually other reptiles, like ichthyosaurs and crocodiles. It is around 20 feet long, which makes it one of the largest reptiles in the ocean.

What makes *Liopleurodon* really scary is not its size, but its massive head, which is over 3 feet long and packed with nearly a hundred knife-sharp teeth.

SCALE

Metriorhynchus: Unlike other species of Jurassic crocodile, which paddle in lagoons and rivers, *Metriorhynchus* enjoys swimming far out into the ocean.

Perfectly suited for living in the sea, *Metriorhynchus* has a long and skinny body that can glide through the water like an eel, flippers on its hands and feet, and a big fin on its tail that propels it forward. Don't try to get into a race with *Metriorhynchus* because it can swim much, much faster than you.

Plesiosaurus: When you spot the mighty *Plesiosaurus*, you relax. It looks like a sauropod dinosaur dropped into the water, with a tiny head, long neck, and big belly. Surely this won't hurt you? Wrong. *Plesiosaurus* is a meat-eater!

Well adapted for living in the ocean, *Plesiosaurus* has four huge flippers that help it swim, and long, sharp teeth for preying on fish, squid, and other seafood.

Rhomaleosaurus: One of the closest cousins of *Liopleurodon* is another bloodthirsty beast, *Rhomaleosaurus*. Both species are members of the pliosaur group: large-headed, sharp-toothed, fast-swimming meat-eaters that rule the waves.

As you swim, you keep your eyes open, watching for *Rhomaleosaurus*, ready to swim for your life if you see it...

Dearcmhara: You need to be really lucky to spot *Dearcmhara*. This fast-swimming, fish-eating reptile is a close cousin of *Ichthyosaurus* and *Temnodontosaurus*. But it is very shy, and lives in only the coldest parts of the ocean.

Unlike *Ichthyosaurus*, *Temnodontosaurus* is huge! It is 33 feet long, bigger than many boats. Because it is so big it needs to eat more than just fish, so it feeds on other sea reptiles as well, including smaller ichthyosaurs!

Temnodontosaurus: *Temnodontosaurus* is another ichthyosaur and looks a lot like *Ichthyosaurus*. It has a long snout, many small teeth, a fin on its back, and flippers. It can also swim very fast.

The first birds

The skies are a lot more interesting in the Jurassic than in the Triassic. In the Triassic there were no birds, but our feathered friends make their first appearance in the middle part of the Jurassic. When you look up, you see them flapping and fluttering through the air, munching on insects and fighting with the much larger pterosaurs.

Xiaotingia: This little guy is the size of a crow. It's a troodontid, a type of dinosaur that is very closely related to birds. *Xiaotingia* has feathers all over its body, long arms turned into wings, and a beak that it uses to grab its prey.

As you look through your binoculars at a flock of *Xiaotingia* in the distance, you can't really tell the difference between them and birds. That's because they differ in only some small details of their bones that you can't see with the naked eye.

Campylognathoides: This pterosaur looks similar to its cousins *Dimorphodon* and *Dorygnathus*. It is about the same size, with a wingspan of almost 5 feet. It also has a large skull with sharp teeth, perfect for catching insects.

What sets *Campylognathoides* apart from other pterosaurs is its huge eyes. This is a flying animal with incredible vision. It can see swarms of insects from far away, and can even hunt at night when light levels are low.

SCALE

Dimorphodon: This pterosaur flaps its 5-foot wide wings with great power, pushing it through the sky as it chases swarms of insects.

It has a big skull full of sharp teeth, and snaps its jaws quickly in order to catch its prey. It needs to move fast, because insects can fly, too, and if *Dimorphodon* is too slow it won't have any dinner tonight.

Eosinopteryx: A feathery little creature flutters above your head. It's about a foot long, and it has wings and a beak. It looks a lot like *Anchiornis*, and also looks like *Xiaotingia*, but is smaller. What you're looking at is yet another species of very birdlike troodontid dinosaur: *Eosinopteryx*.

Anchiornis: The pigeon-sized *Anchiornis* is a close cousin of *Xiaotingia*. It is also a troodontid dinosaur that is covered in feathers and looks like a bird.

Anchiornis is beautiful, with feathers of many different colors. Gray feathers coat most of the body, the wings are made up of black and white quill-pens, and the head has a reddish-orange crown.

Dorygnathus: You turn your head in disgust as you put down your binoculars. There is no other way to put it: the flying animal you have just seen is ugly. It kind of looks like a big furry bat. This is *Dorygnathus*, a type of pterosaur.

Dorygnathus might not be pretty, but it's well adapted to catching prey. The very long front teeth mesh together when the jaw closes, trapping any fish caught inside.

As you've journeyed through the Early–Middle Jurassic, you'll have seen dinosaurs eating all kinds of food. But did you realize that each dinosaur has specially adapted features that help it eat its food of choice? Read these field notes and look back at your journey to learn how dinosaurs get their dinner in the Early–Middle Jurassic.

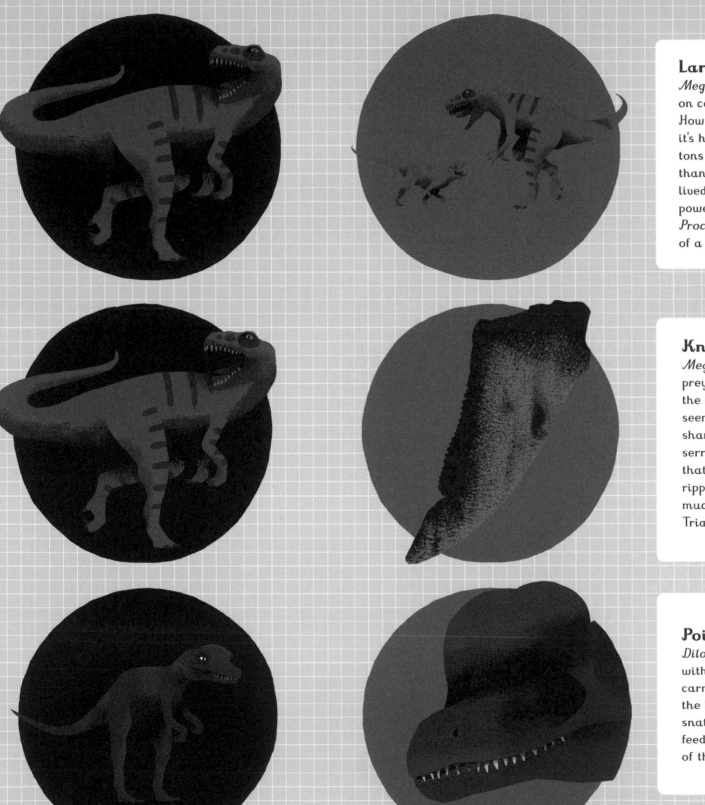

Large size

Megalosaurus is a predator who relies on catching and eating other dinosaurs. How does it do this? One answer is that it's huge! At 30 feet long and nearly two tons in weight, it is considerably larger than any meat-eating dinosaur that lived in the Triassic. Its large size gives it power and strength to catch its prey, like *Proceratosaurus*, which is only the size of a human.

Knife-shaped teeth

Megalosaurus can eat all kinds of prey with its specialized teeth. It has the classic knife-shaped teeth that are seen in many theropods. They are thin, sharp, and curved, and have tiny little serrations on the front and back sides that act like saw blades, perfect for ripping into flesh. And they are big— much bigger than the teeth of earlier Triassic theropods.

Pointy snout

Dilophosaurus has a long snout, packed with sharp teeth, like many other carnivores. Why? The longer the snout the better, as a long snout is useful for snatching up speedy prey. Also, while feeding, it helps dig deeper into the flesh of the animal.

Plant-eating skull

Scelidosaurus is not a very strong animal. It doesn't have big jaw muscles, meaning that it can't bite very hard, unlike *Megalosaurus*. However, the skull of *Scelidosaurus* is well adapted for its diet. It has a beak at the front of the snout for grabbing plants, and long rows of triangle-shaped teeth for cutting up stems and leaves.

Huge hands

Heterodontosaurus is a small plant-eating dinosaur with huge hands. Each hand has five fingers, just like a human. The muscles on the hands allow the fingers to come together strongly and grab things, like we can. *Heterodontosaurus* uses its hands to pull leaves and stems off trees, then shoves this food into its mouth.

Small head

Shunosaurus is a huge dinosaur, growing up to 30 feet long, so you'd think it would have a huge head, right? Wrong. The head is tiny compared with its body. This is because it doesn't need to be any bigger. *Shunosaurus* doesn't need huge jaws for biting into prey. Instead, it bites off leaves, swallows them, and lets its big belly digest everything.

The early part of the Jurassic is a time of fierce battles. As you travel, you'll see meat-eaters stalking their prey and the prey species protecting themselves with plates, or fighting back with tail clubs or teeth of their own. Use these notes to help you understand the weapons and armor you've seen in the Early-Middle Jurassic Period.

Running machines

You don't want to get into a race with the meat-eating theropods of the Early-Middle Jurassic, because they will chase you down and eat you. Many of them can run at speeds of over 25 miles an hour. They can run so fast because their bodies are lightweight and they have long, strong legs like a sprinter. Walking on only two legs makes them faster than dinosaurs that walk on all four.

Head crests

Let's face it, many of the meat-eating theropods of the Early-Middle Jurassic are strange looking. Take *Monolophosaurus*: it has a big crest sticking up from the top of its head, kind of like a Mohawk haircut. But this crest is made out of bone, not hair. Like *Cryolophosaurus* and *Dilophosaurus*, *Monolophosaurus* uses its crest for display purposes: to intimidate its rivals or attract female mates.

Hunting in packs

Do you think a sharp-clawed, knife-toothed, fast-running theropod is scary? Then imagine a bunch of them hunting together. Some small theropods, the raptor dinosaurs, live in packs. Hopefully this is something that you'll never come across, because if you do, it may be the last thing you ever see ...

Tusklike teeth

If you're a plant-eater, it's not just predators you have to watch out for. *Heterodontosaurus* has two teeth, one on each side of the front part of the lower jaw, that are much bigger and sharper than the others. These are called tusks. *Heterodontosaurus* is a plant-eater, so it doesn't use its tusks to eat meat. Instead, it uses them to fight rivals over food or territory.

Tail clubs

Stay away from *Shunosaurus*. Sure, this big sauropod is a plant-eater, so you don't have to worry about it trying to eat you. But sometimes theropods try to eat *Shunosaurus*, and that's when things get nasty. *Shunosaurus* has a bony club with two spikes at the end of its tail. Whenever it's scared it will swing its tail, and you don't want to get in the way of this powerful weapon!

Hip spikes

This stegosaur has big triangular plates all along its neck, back, and tail. But over the hips, one set of plates is replaced by something bigger and sharper: two pointy spikes. One spike is on the left side, the other on the right side. *Huayangosaurus* will twist its hips and thrust these spikes into any predators that try to take a bite.

Ancient giant: *Cetiosaurus*

The sauropods are the biggest dinosaurs of all and some of them were the largest land animals to have ever lived, growing to 100 feet long and weighing over 65 tons! That's three times longer than a bus and as heavy as five fully grown elephants. As you've noticed when traveling through the Early-Middle Jurassic, sauropods like *Cetiosaurus* pictured here, have begun to grow to these giant, earth-shaking sizes. Sauropods are some of the most distinctive dinosaurs, and all have these common features to help them survive.

Size
Though *Cetiosaurus* isn't as big as sauropods of the Late Jurassic like *Brachiosaurus* will be, it is still an ancient giant at 53 to 59 feet long. Its thigh bone is almost 6 feet in length. That's as long as a fully grown man! Its huge size helps protect it from predators. *Cetiosaurus* also travels in herds for more protection.

Quadropeds
All sauropods walk on four legs, which are strong and muscular. They look like columns. Just like how columns hold up a building, the thick limbs of sauropods support their massive weight.

Small head
Sauropods have a tiny head at the end of their long necks. Their teeth are simple and they cannot chew their food very well. Instead, they use their heads like a vacuum cleaner: to grab as many stems and leaves as they can, as quickly as they can.

Long neck
All sauropods have a long neck like *Cetiosaurus*. They use their neck to help them get food. All sauropods are plant-eaters. Their long necks help them reach high into the trees, giving them access to plants that no other dinosaurs can reach.

Big belly
The big belly of sauropods helps them to digest their food. Because they can't chew their food very well, and because plants are difficult to digest, they need to keep plants in their stomach for a long time (sometimes several weeks!) to digest every last little bit of nutrition from them.

Meat-eaters eat high-protein, high-fat food, so they don't need to keep it in their stomachs for so long to get out all of the nutrients.

WELCOME TO THE LATE
JURASSIC

It's 150 million years ago. You're deep in a forest, smelling the strong, sweet scent of the pine trees, feeling peaceful and calm as you watch the plate-backed *Stegosaurus* guzzling some bushes and shrubs close to the ground. But suddenly, out of nowhere comes the horned *Ceratosaurus*, on the hunt for a dinosaur for its dinner. The *Stegosaurus* isn't going to go down without a fight. Just in time, you crouch flat on the ground as it swings its huge tail, striking the meat-eater with its spikes. *Ceratosaurus* roars with anger and snaps with its huge jaws. You back away as the battle continues.

Welcome to the Late Jurassic . . .

The golden age

You're seeing more kinds of herbivores than ever before! Many different species of huge long-necked sauropods thunder across the land, making the ground shake around you. But they are not the only plant-eaters. Living underneath them are many smaller species, including amazing dinosaurs covered in plates and spikes for protection. As you continue on your way one thing becomes pretty clear: the Late Jurassic is the golden age of plant-eating dinosaurs.

Diplodocus: Though it's another long-necked sauropod, you notice that *Diplodocus* is quite different from *Brachiosaurus* and *Brontosaurus*. It is smaller and more lightly built, and only weighs about 16 and a half tons.

Diplodocus doesn't use its long neck to reach high into the trees, but sticks it out like a crane, scooping up small plants and bushes near the ground. Because it doesn't need to reach high up, its back legs are longer than its front ones, unlike *Brachiosaurus*.

Camptosaurus: *Camptosaurus* looks boring compared to other dinosaurs. It doesn't have big teeth, or a long neck, or armor, or spikes. But it is good at one thing: eating plants.

Camptosaurus is much faster than the sauropods, so can outrace them to new sources of its food: ferns and small trees.

Brachiosaurus: When you see *Brachiosaurus*, you think it looks more like a monument than an animal. This sauropod stands tall and proud. Its front legs are a little longer than its back legs to make it even taller, and it has the standard long neck of any sauropod. It weighs about 60 tons, more than seven elephants!

Stegosaurus: There is no mistaking *Stegosaurus*. You can recognize this dinosaur from a distance, because it has one really distinctive feature: a set of big plates sticking up from its back.

Other dinosaurs know to stay away from *Stegosaurus*'s impossible-to-bite-through bony plates and spiky tail.

Mamenchisaurus: This dinosaur has the longest neck of any animal you've ever seen. It's nearly 30 feet long! When *Mamenchisaurus* sticks its neck high into the canopy, it can reach leaves that no other dinosaur can access.

SCALE

46

Brontosaurus: This dinosaur is the most famous of all of the sauropods. Its name means "thunder lizard," and often this is used as a nickname for all the sauropods. It is a fitting name because each time its feet hit the ground, they bring with them the force of more than 33 tons of weight. You can hear *Brontosaurus* approaching for miles.

Gargoyleosaurus: This dinosaur is named after gargoyles, those strange carvings of mythical animals on the roofs of many old churches. This is a fitting name, because *Gargoyleosaurus* looks like something out of a fairy tale. It is a grotesque animal: about 13 feet long, weighing nearly a ton, covered in bony armor and horns that protect it from meat-eaters.

Dragons and killer chickens

You're so busy looking at all the amazing plant-eaters that you forget a crucial rule in the day of the dinosaurs: where there are herbivores, there are usually predators lurking, waiting to pounce. And sure enough, there are many meat-eating theropod dinosaurs in the Late Jurassic world. Some of these rule the top of the food chain, dominating all other dinosaurs by virtue of their enormous size. But others are small, fast-running carnivores that make a living hunting small mammals and lizards living in the bushes.

Allosaurus: You move carefully through the forest, on the lookout for one animal in particular ... The famous *Allosaurus* is the king of the Late Jurassic, able to hunt the biggest sauropods. This big-headed carnivore lurks around every corner, waiting to pounce on unsuspecting prey with its 6-inch claws. It's a large, powerful animal: about 35 feet long and weighing a couple of tons. And there are many of them around. You need to watch your back!

Compsognathus: There's something tiny running toward you. *Compsognathus* is like a killer chicken. The "chicken" part of its nickname is funny, and very fitting, because this little meat-eater isn't much bigger than a rooster.

But *Compsognathus* is fast and fierce, and you realize the "killer" part of its nickname isn't anything to laugh at as it snaps at your ankles like an angry dog.

SCALE

Ceratosaurus: *Allosaurus* is at the top of the food chain, but living alongside it is another fearsome predator about half the size. This is *Ceratosaurus*, another dinosaur you don't want to mess with. It may not be as big or strong as *Allosaurus*, but it is much faster, because it has a lighter skeleton and longer legs. With horns on its head, it looks like a dragon.

Ornitholestes: There are so many big predators in the Late Jurassic. But while *Allosaurus*, *Torvosaurus*, and *Ceratosaurus* fight for the large prey, you see *Ornitholestes* quietly stalking through the bushes, jumping out to grab small lizards, frogs, and birds.

Usually *Ornitholestes* is nothing to fear. But when it gets really hungry, it will go after larger prey. So beware.

Limusaurus: Little *Limusaurus* is one weird dinosaur. It is one of the closest cousins of *Ceratosaurus*. But it looks so different. It is much smaller, only about the size of a golden retriever.

Torvosaurus: Here's a survival tip for staying alive in the Late Jurassic. If you see a *Torvosaurus*, be sure to keep your distance. Believe it or not, this monstrous meat-eater is a little bigger than the great *Allosaurus*, with huge jaws, sharp teeth, and slashing claws.

Thankfully, *Torvosaurus* is a rare animal. You probably will go months or years without ever seeing one. But don't get lazy and forget about it, because if you do …

Across the Atlantic

There are many oceans for you to cool off in on your journey through the Late Jurassic. As the pieces of land that will become Europe and North America separate from each other, the Atlantic Ocean is getting wider. The seas are full of life. There are thousands of species of fish, and lots of swimming animals with spiral shells called ammonites. But be careful. Ruling this world are many types of big reptiles: ichthyosaurs, plesiosaurs, and some of the fiercest crocodiles to ever live.

Pliosaurus: As you enter the water, you're on the lookout for *Pliosaurus*. This monster is at the top of the ocean food chain. It is a 33-foot long predator with a skull longer than an adult man, full of thick, sharp teeth that can crush bone.

A Pliosaurus could swallow you in a single gulp. So if you think there is any chance one may be lurking, get out of the water immediately!

Kimmerosaurus: You're hoping you'll see *Kimmerosaurus*. It lives out in the deep ocean, far from the shores, so it is very hard to spot one, and we don't know much about it.

Reports say that it has a big belly, a long neck, four flippers for swimming, and a skull full of tiny thin teeth that it uses to catch fish.

SCALE

Machimosaurus: As you come out of the water on to the beach, you see *Machimosaurus*—a crocodile—eating a turtle! It is big, about 25 feet long.

The jaws of *Machimosaurus* are lined with teeth that look like thick pegs, covered with lots of little points and ridges and spikes, perfect for breaking the hard shells of turtles. Best to keep your distance from this croc.

Dakosaurus: *Dakosaurus* is a crocodile that is different from any crocodile you've ever heard of. It doesn't live on land but out in the ocean. And it has a massive skull that looks like the head of a *T. rex*, with huge jaw muscles and super-sharp teeth that can rip through flesh. *Dakosaurus* is a top predator, and you can think of it as a crocodile version of a shark or killer whale.

Brachypterygius: A little later you spot *Brachypterygius*, another type of ichthyosaur. It is a close cousin of *Ophthalmosaurus*, but its eyes are much smaller.

Brachypterygius can't see as well as *Ophthalmosaurus* in the deep waters, so it spends its time closer to the surface, chasing after schools of fish.

Ophthalmosaurus: My, what big eyes you have! That's the first thing you think when you gaze at *Ophthalmosaurus*. The eyes of this ichthyosaur are bigger than your head!

Ophthalmosaurus dives deep into the water to hunt for fish, using its large eyes to help it see in the darkness of the ocean bottom.

51

Flying terrors

As well as fearing what's waiting in the bushes, it's time to be scared of what's above you. Birds and pterosaurs sail through the Late Jurassic skies. They fight over food and sometimes eat each other. And some of these winged creatures are really frightening: they're big, with sharp teeth and claws. Be sure to always watch the sky above, because one of these flying terrors could swoop down and attack.

Archaeopteryx: You see a crow-sized creature and wonder if it's another troodontid. Nope, this is *Archaeopteryx*, one of the first birds.

Archaeopteryx can fly, but not very well. Its chest muscles—which power its wings—are much smaller than those of other birds.

Batrachognathus: *Batrachognathus* is a pterosaur with a scary smile. Its huge mouth is full of tiny spear-shaped teeth. But you don't need to worry. This is one pterosaur that won't hurt you.

Batrachognathus eats insects, gulping down dragonflies and other bugs into its big mouth and then crunching them up with its many teeth.

Sordes: *Sordes* is a small fuzzball of a pterosaur. It has the classic large bat-like wings and long tails of many pterosaurs, but its body is covered in a soft and fuzzy substance that looks and feels like hair. This helps keep *Sordes* warm during the winters.

Rhamphorhynchus: Something glides past you quickly. It must be a pterosaur. But what kind? After consulting your field guide to pterosaurs you realize it's *Rhamphorhynchus*.

Rhamphorhynchus has a long tail with something sticking out from the end, like a small diamond-shaped wing. This helps it keep its balance while flying.

SCALE

Ctenochasma: It looks like a cross between a bat and a pelican. What could it possibly be? It's *Ctenochasma*, a pterosaur that flaps through the air on its big wings.

Ctenochasma eats shrimps and bugs with its bizarre teeth. How bizarre? It has over four hundred tiny teeth, which are packed tightly together. When the jaw snaps shut, these teeth become a net, trapping the minuscule prey inside.

Pterodactylus: Swarming like a flock of seagulls above the lake are thousands of *Pterodactylus*. These are small pterosaurs, with wings that are 3 feet wide at most.

Some *Pterodactylus* you see are smaller than others. Could these be a different species? No—they are babies and teenagers. These flocks are made up of *Pterodactylus* of all ages, living together for protection.

You've seen with your own eyes that the Late Jurassic is a dinosaur-eat-dinosaur world. Big predators, like *Allosaurus* and *Torvosaurus*, have their choice of many prey species, like *Diplodocus* and *Stegosaurus*. These prey species eat all kinds of plants—big pine trees, small shrubs called cycads, and many kinds of ferns. Use these notes to find out how different dinosaurs get their food in the Late Jurassic.

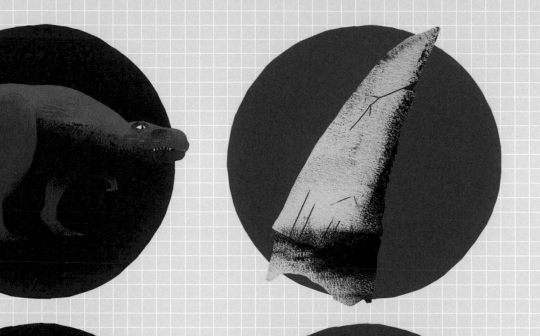

Teeth

Torvosaurus has some of the largest teeth of any dinosaur that ever lived. They are so big that you can't fit one in your hand. Not only are these teeth big, but they are very sharp, perfect for ripping into prey. Imagine a mouth full of these teeth trying to eat you ...

Useful hands

While *Torvosaurus* uses its big jaws to catch prey, *Ornitholestes* uses its jaws and its hands. Its hands have three fingers with claws, and it uses all of them to grab its prey such as small lizards and early mammals. *Ornitholestes* then eats these animals using its small, pointy teeth.

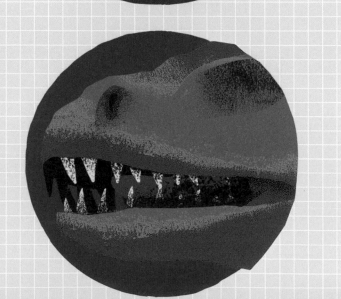

Sniffing out dinner

Allosaurus was a terrifying predator at the top of the food chain. But how did it know when to pounce? As well as using its sight and hearing, it had a good sense of smell, which it used to sniff out tasty dinosaurs on the move. It then probably hid in bushes and jumped out on prey walking by. Later dinosaurs, like *T. rex* and *Velociraptor*, developed an even better sense of smell than the mighty *Allosaurus*.

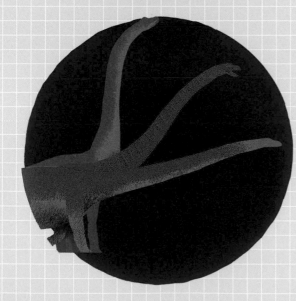

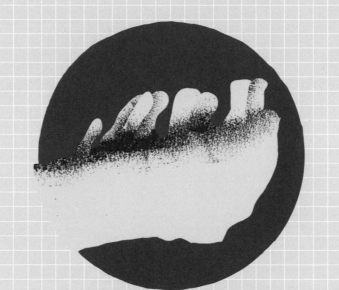

Grab and grind

The dog-sized *Chilesaurus* is a very close cousin of *Allosaurus*. But wow does it look different. Not only is it smaller, but its teeth look like little spoons, not like the knife-shaped teeth of *Allosaurus*. The teeth of *Chilesaurus* are not very good at cutting up meat, but they are the perfect shape for grabbing and grinding plants. So *Chilesaurus* is a theropod, but a plant-eating one!

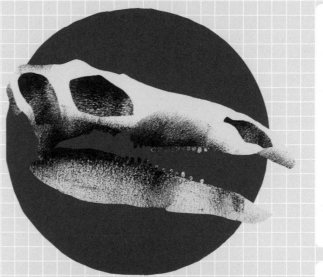

Special skull

Stegosaurus is most famous for the big plates on its back. But it also has a really distinctive skull, which helps it eat a lot of plants. The skull is long, like the head of a horse. There is a beak at the front, which is used to grab leaves and branches. Behind the beak are many small leaf-shaped teeth. These are used to grind up the plants before they are swallowed.

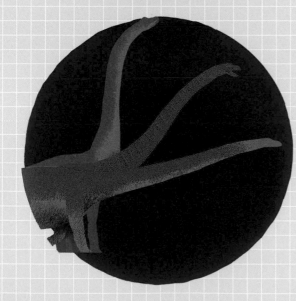

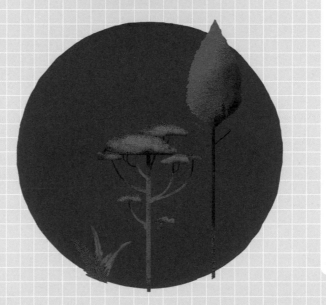

Reaching high and low

Many different species of huge, big-bellied, long-necked sauropods live in the Late Jurassic. How do they get along with each other? Because they have different necks. Some are really long and can reach high into the forest. Others are shorter and can reach smaller trees. And other species, like *Diplodocus*, have necks that can't reach very high at all, so eat plants close to the ground. All these sauropods eat different plants, so they can live together happily.

As you've journeyed through the Late Jurassic you've seen some huge battles between terrifying meat-eaters and sometimes equally fearsome herbivores. Have you noticed the different ways in which dinosaurs attack and defend themselves? Look out for the many weapons and sets of armor in these field notes to understand more.

Slash and grab

Allosaurus is a big carnivore that kind of looks like *T. rex*, although there is one major difference: its arms are much longer, and have three fingers capped with sharp claws. *Allosaurus* uses these claws to hunt and rip apart its prey before shoving it into its mouth.

Horn strike

Ceratosaurus has a horn sticking out of its nose. This is not for defense, because *Ceratosaurus* is a strong, fast-running, mighty carnivore that fears little. No, it uses its horn for two things: as an offensive weapon to strike prey and a display feature to attract mates.

Balancing act

Why does *Compsognathus* have a tail that's bigger than its torso? Because it helps the small dinosaur keep its balance so it can run faster and move quickly in different directions—important weapons when hunting speedy lizard prey!

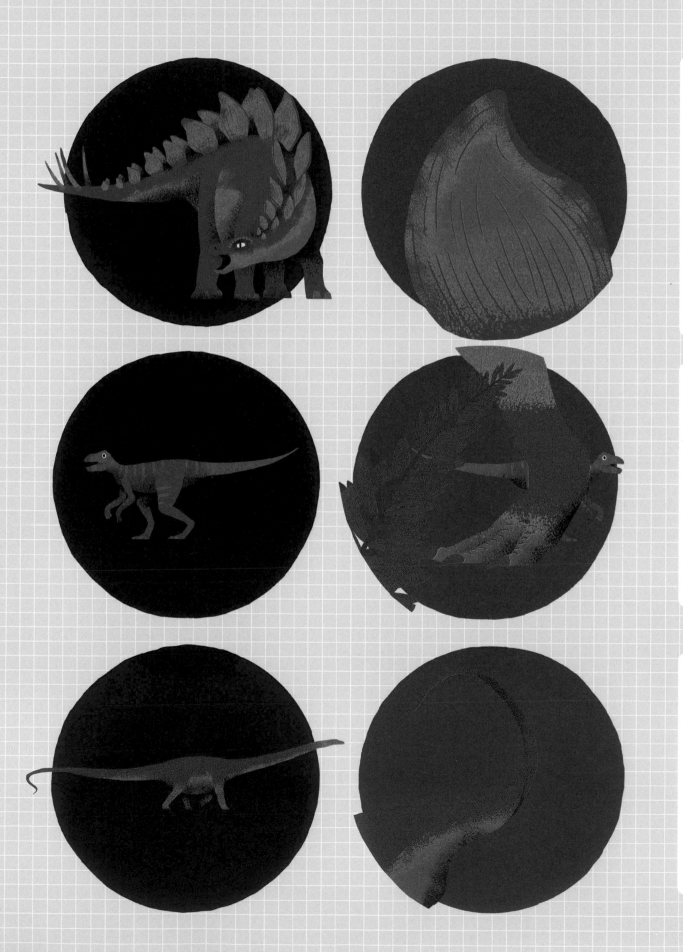

Colorful plates

Does *Stegosaurus* also use its back plates for defense? Sometimes, yes. If an *Allosaurus* tries to take a bite out of the *Stegosaurus's* back then it will break its teeth on the plates. But this is not their primary purpose. The main reason *Stegosaurus* has these big, beautiful plates is for display. A *Stegosaurus* with bigger, more colorful plates looks more attractive to its mates and scarier and stronger to its rivals in the herd.

Teeny tiny

Blink and you'll miss *Fruitadens*. This pint-sized plant-eater is one of the smallest dinosaurs in the world. It is only just over 1 and a half feet long and weighs less than half a pound. Being so small has one major advantage for *Fruitadens*: in a world full of dangerous predators like *Allosaurus*, it can easily hide and escape.

Whip lash

Sauropods like *Diplodocus* don't want to cause you trouble. All they want to do is stand around and eat plants all day. But if a predator gets too close, then *Diplodocus* will use an unusual weapon. Its long, skinny tail can be swung like a whip. Even the biggest and fiercest predators, like *Torvosaurus* and *Allosaurus*, know to fear the whiplash tail of *Diplodocus*.

Early bird: *Archaeopteryx*

Maybe the most special dinosaurs are animals that you didn't know were dinosaurs at all: birds. Yes, birds are dinosaurs. They are a group of mostly small, large-armed, feathered dinosaurs that can fly. They are dinosaurs in the same way that a bat is a strange type of mammal that can fly. So what does it mean to be a bird? All birds share many important features, which are illustrated here on one of the oldest and most primitive birds of all, the Late Jurassic *Archaeopteryx*.

Eggs
All birds reproduce by laying eggs. This is something they inherited from their dinosaur ancestors. All dinosaurs laid eggs, too!

Quill-pen feathers
All birds have feathers. Quill-pen feathers are big and found on the arms. They have a central shaft and many small, soft barbs coming out of the shaft on both sides. This gives these feathers the classic shape of a quill pen. There are several layers of these feathers on the arms, which together make up the wing. It is the wing that makes birds able to fly.

Gripping claws
Many birds live in trees. They have claws on their feet that help them grip on to the branches. This is called perching.

Down feathers
Other feathers are small and simple, and kind of look like hair. They cover the body. These are called down feathers. They help birds keep warm.

Large wings
The wings of birds are really big compared to the body. This is partly caused by the many layers of feathers. But it is also caused by the long length of the arm. Compared to all other dinosaurs, birds have incredibly long arms that are longer than the legs, and often even longer than the body!

Dinosaur or bird?
Early birds like *Archaeopteryx* look a lot like today's birds, but they are different in some ways. *Archaeopteryx* has teeth, sharp claws on its hands, and a long tail, which are features seen in dinosaurs like *Velociraptor* or *Allosaurus*, but not in modern birds. So in many ways, *Archaeopteryx* is a cross between a prehistoric dinosaur and a bird you might see today!

Varied diet
Birds eat all kinds of food. Some are herbivores, some are carnivores (some of which are known now as "birds of prey") and most are somewhere in between. They all have a beak at the front of their snout, which they use to grab and cut their food.

Hollow bones
The skeletons of birds are very light. This is because many of their bones are hollow. A light body makes it easier for birds to fly. As you can imagine, it takes a lot more energy to fly if your body is big and bulky.

WELCOME TO THE
CRETACEOUS

It's 66 million years ago. You're looking at a river, its crystal-blue water making a whooshing sound as it comes down from the mountains in the distance. An *Edmontosaurus* is stripping off flowers by the riverside, carefully chewing each mouthful. Off in the distance, a herd of *Triceratops* is snacking on smaller ferns growing near the ground. But you can sense that something isn't right. Out of the corner of your eye you see a flash of something, and then hear a mighty roar. A *Tyrannosaurus rex* has sprinted out of the trees, dashing at full speed toward the *Edmontosaurus*. It leaps toward its prey and sinks its teeth in, bringing it to the ground.

Welcome to the Cretaceous . . .

Flower feeders

As you travel through the Cretaceous forest, you notice colorful plants that you've never seen before in the prehistoric world . . . flowers! These have only recently evolved, and—along with the leaves and stems of trees, and ferns and bushes—provide food for the many different species of herbivores in the Cretaceous. And sure enough, soon you see huge long-necked sauropods, horned dinosaurs, and even duckbilled species, all on the lookout for lunch.

Dreadnoughtus: You are struggling to find the words to describe what's in front of you. It's bigger than anything you've ever seen before. It's over 80 feet long, and its neck stretches higher than a five-story building. This is *Dreadnoughtus*—one of the biggest dinosaurs of all.

Argentinosaurus: After catching a glimpse of the massive *Dreadnoughtus* you thought you would never see something that big again. But you were wrong. As you walk through the forest and come to a gap in the trees, a dinosaur even bigger comes into view.

Argentinosaurus is a species of sauropod closely related to *Dreadnoughtus*. It is nearly 100 feet long and weighs more than 66 tons!

SCALE

Triceratops: There is no mistaking *Triceratops*. This plant-eater is one of the most familiar dinosaurs of all.

Triceratops means "three-horned face," and when you spot one eating some ferns, you see why. It has a small horn on its nose and a long, pointy one over each eye.

Nothronychus: This wacky theropod looks like a dinosaur version of a sloth. It's about the size of a giraffe and moves really slowly. It has a big pot-belly and long arms with skinny, curved claws.

Nothronychus evolved from meat-eating theropods, but it is a gentle plant-eater.

Ankylosaurus: When you live in the same place as *T. rex* you need to do something to protect yourself. Just look at *Ankylosaurus*. This car-sized plant-eater has a body completely covered in thick bony plates. Even the mighty *T. rex* can't bite through the tough armor of an *Ankylosaurus* without breaking its teeth, so it doesn't try.

Parasaurolophus: OOO*MMMMM*PHHHH! OOO*MMMMM*PHHHH! There is a loud, deep noise coming from the trees behind you. When the animal appears you're relieved it's only *Parasaurolophus*, a plant-eater.

To call to its friends, *Parasaurolophus* uses a snorkel-shaped crest on its skull to make trumpeting sounds.

Pachycephalosaurus: When you see a herd of the horse-sized *Pachycephalosaurus*, you realize not all plant-eating dinosaurs are gentle. The males charge at each other full speed, using their thick, bony heads as battering rams. The goal is to knock the other one down. It's like a competition in which the last dinosaur standing wins the respect of the herd.

The mightiest predators

You're enjoying your stroll through the Cretaceous, but a rustle from the bushes makes you jump back in fright. You have good reason to be scared. The biggest, scariest, and nastiest predators of all terrorize the Cretaceous. *Tyrannosaurus rex* is surely the most famous, and the one you definitely want to stay away from. But don't forget about the others. If you spend too much time obsessing about *T. rex* then a pack of *Velociraptors* may sneak up and snatch you away . . .

Deinocheirus: *Deinocheirus* is the weirdest dinosaur you've ever seen. It's huge, about the same size as *T. rex*. It has a big hump on its back, stocky little legs, long arms with massive claws, and a long, skinny head with a beak.

Alvarezsaurus: As you come to a clearing you see something you've never seen before: a dinosaur with its head stuck in the ground. *Alvarezsaurus* eats insects, and so it's sticking its snout into a termite nest for food.

Alvarezsaurus is a fast runner with a slender body and short, stubby arms.

Troodon: The dog-sized *Troodon* moves fast, hides easily, and has such a large brain that it can outsmart any other dinosaur. Luckily for you, it usually picks on small animals, like lizards and frogs. It even eats plants. But you never know when a *Troodon* may decide to hunt something bigger.

Ornithomimus: What's this dinosaur that looks like a big ostrich? It's not a bird, it's *Ornithomimus*—a theropod covered in feathers that runs fast on its long legs.

Ornithomimus doesn't have sharp teeth to eat meat. In fact, it has no teeth at all. Instead, it has a beak, which it uses to eat bugs, shellfish, and plants.

Tyrannosaurus: Here's one creature you're really hoping you don't see on your journey. *T. rex* is the undisputed ruler of the Cretaceous world.

T. rex is a monster more than 40 feet long, weighing almost 8 tons! It will eat whatever it wants, whenever it wants.

SCALE

Velociraptor: *Velociraptor* can kill you in so many ways. It has a skull full of razor-sharp teeth, piercing claws on its hands, and an enormous sickle-shaped claw on its foot. It can outrun you, too, and it's one of the smartest dinosaurs.

Brain and brawn, *Velociraptor* has it all. That's why you should fear this little predator almost as much as the great *T. rex*.

Monsters of the deep

As you come across another beach, you realize that it's hard to avoid water in the Cretaceous. The world is divided up into many small continents, which are separated by vast oceans. Shallow seas also cover much of the land. But you need to be careful as you're crossing the water. These are prime environments for sea monsters, many species of reptiles that rule the waves.

Platypterygius: You hear something that sounds like a slap. Something is hitting the water. As you squint your eyes you can see a *Platypterygius* in the distance.

This 20-foot-long ichthyosaur has a set of huge, wing-like front flippers. It uses these flippers as paddles, allowing it to move quickly through the water. When the big flipper hits the water it makes quite a noise!

Kronosaurus: Its name strikes fear into your heart. *Kronosaurus*. This beast is over 30 feet long and has a head that is bigger than a human, full of sharp teeth that are the size of bananas.

Stay far, far away from *Kronosaurus*. It usually eats turtles, squids, and other ocean-living reptiles. But it would eat you, too.

Elasmosaurus: Wow! *Elasmosaurus* has the longest neck of any animal you've ever seen. Its neck is even longer than the necks of some of the big land-living dinosaurs, like *Diplodocus* and *Brontosaurus*. *Elasmosaurus* uses its stretched neck like a dart to quickly grab fish for its dinner.

SCALE

Malawania: As you look out into the sea, a graceful reptile leaps out of the water, glides for a few moments through the air, and then dives back into the waves.

Malawania is a fast-swimming ichthyosaur that uses its long snout to snatch tasty fish.

Archelon: *Archelon* looks like any normal turtle: it has a thick shell covering its body, with a small head sticking out from the front. But *Archelon* is much larger than any turtle you've seen before. It is about 13 feet long, with big flippers that it uses to swim.

Mosasaurus: When you first see *Mosasaurus* you are confused. It looks like a weird combination of a crocodile and a shark, but it's neither of these animals. It's a close cousin of lizards, right down to its scaly skin.

Mosasaurus is almost 60 feet long! Because it is so big, it can eat almost anything it wants, including you if you swim too close to it ...

Swooping giants

As you're walking through the Cretaceous forests you need to look out for *T. rex* and *Velociraptor*. But don't forget about what might be above you. The Cretaceous skies are alive with many birds and pterosaurs. Some are small and cute, others are big and scaly, and some are even the size of small airplanes! Avoid open spaces so you don't get snatched from above!

Male *Confuciusornis* have long ribbon-shaped feathers on the tail to attract the females, who just have a stubby tail without feathers.

Confuciusornis: It's a beautiful sight: a flock of *Confuciusornis* soaring majestically in the air. These crow-sized birds are gorgeous, with feathers in alternating bands of red, black, and gray.

Dsungaripterus: You start to feel nervous when you see a flock of *Dsungaripterus* flying above you. These pterosaurs are fairly large, with wingspans of more than 9 feet.

What really worries you is *Dsungaripterus's* spooky head. Its jaws are long and skinny, and taper to a sharp point at the front, like a giant pair of tweezers! But don't be scared. It uses these jaws to pick up small prey like crabs and bugs.

Pterodaustro: What is that strange winged animal standing in the water, sticking its head in the currents like a flamingo? It's *Pterodaustro*, an unusual pterosaur.

Pterodaustro has a big head full of tiny thin teeth that look like the bristles on a comb. These are perfect for catching tiny little bugs and shellfish in the water.

SCALE

Quetzalcoatlus: The sky suddenly grows dark as *Quetzalcoatlus* soars overhead. This pterosaur has wings that stretch for almost 32 feet, which makes it larger than many small airplanes!

Quetzalcoatlus is the largest flying animal that has ever lived.

Vegavis: There's a bird floating on the water, bobbing up and down with the gentle waves. This is *Vegavis*, an ancestor of ducks and geese.

Vegavis kind of looks like a duck. It is about the same size, and has the same wide bill at the front of its mouth, to filter little shrimps and sea bugs from the water.

Microraptor: You're standing underneath a tall pine tree when you hear a sound from above. You look up and see a fluffy dinosaur slowly parachuting down from the treetop, its arms and legs spread out to break its fall. This is *Microraptor*, a chicken-sized dinosaur with feathery wings on its arms, legs, and tail.

Yi: Little *Yi* is the dinosaur version of a bat. This critter has a broad flap of skin stretching between its fingers and its body. The flap is even supported by a toothpick-shaped piece of bone. As you observe *Yi* through your binoculars, it suddenly takes flight and you understand what this flap is for: it's a wing!

Early on your walk through the Cretaceous, you saw a *T. rex* bring down an *Edmontosaurus*. These are two of the most successful dinosaurs of the Cretaceous, but one is a predator and one is a plant-eater. These notes show how they have adapted to eat the food that they do.

T. rex is one of the greatest predators in the history of earth and one of the biggest meat-eaters to ever live on land, measuring over 40 feet in length, standing almost 10 feet tall, and weighing over 8 tons. Not only is *T. rex* big, but it has one of the strongest bites of any animal in history.

Huge head

T. rex has a massive head. It is about as long as an average adult human is tall. The skull bones are also very thick, and some of them, like the bones on top of the snout, are strongly fused together. This means *T. rex* is able to bite hard and crunch through bone without hurting itself.

Massive teeth

The 50 teeth of *T. rex* are remarkable weapons. Many of them are over 11 inches long! Not only are the teeth sharp with serrated edges like saw blades, but they are also thick, so they can crush bone without easily breaking.

To kill its prey, *T. rex* would have bit deep and powerfully into an animal, then pulled back, creating long cuts and even making marks on the bones.

Powerful jaw

The jaw muscles of *T. rex* are enormous, bigger than those in any other meat-eating dinosaur. These muscles power the amazing bite strength of *T. rex* and explain why the arms of *T. rex* are so tiny: it's the head, not the claws, that does all the work!

T. rex has a joint between the bones of the lower jaw that allows it to gape wide, meaning it can fit in large prey or animals that are struggling to escape.

The duck-billed *Edmontosaurus* is a plant-eating machine that grows to large sizes, from 30 to 40 feet long. It is such a successful animal that it's the most common herbivore of them all at the end of the Cretaceous period. There are many dinosaurs in the Cretaceous, so how do so many *Edmontosaurus* manage to grow so big? The answer is that they have evolved special features to grab and eat their food.

Duckbill

Edmontosaurus is a member of the Hadrosauridae or "duck-billed" family of dinosaurs, because of the bony beak at the front of its head. This snaps shut to grab food like leaves and stems off of trees. Many other dinosaurs belonged to the same family, including *Parasaurolophus*.

Jaw scissors

Behind its bill, *Edmontosaurus* has thousands of teeth in its mouth, which are packed together into what are called "dental batteries."

The teeth are so tightly packed that they form a single sharp cutting surface, kind of like a knife blade. As the top and bottom jaws come together, the blades slide past each other like a pair of scissors. These "jaw scissors" are a great tool for chewing through plants very quickly.

Bendy neck

The neck of *Edmontosaurus* is flexible, meaning it can turn in lots of different directions. This allows the head to reach all the food in its area, so *Edmontosaurus* gets a bigger dinner! And what does *Edmontosaurus* eat? It has a taste for a new type of plant that started to become very common in the Cretaceous: flowers, including magnolias, sycamores, and palms!

The Cretaceous is a wild time, with so many dinosaurs of different sizes and shapes and diets living all across the world. But lots of dinosaurs means there is competition for food if you're a meat-eater, or lots of dinosaurs trying to eat you if you're a plant-eater. To survive, these dinosaurs have amazing weapons that they use to catch prey, or protect themselves from predators.

Gut slasher
One of the deadliest weapons possessed by any dinosaur is the long, sharp, curved claw on the second toe of *Velociraptor*. This is a weapon you never want to see up close. What does *Velociraptor* do with this scary claw? It uses it first to hold down its victims, and then to slash open their guts.

Smarty pants
Don't get into a game of wits with *Troodon*. Sure, *Troodon* is just a dinosaur, but it's a really smart one. It might even outsmart you. Its brain is so big that it fills most of its head. It's one of the smartest dinosaurs around, and uses its intelligence to help it to attack its prey.

Fish dinner
Baryonyx is a fish-eater. How can you tell? First of all, it has a skull with lots of sharp, conical teeth. The skull is long, so there's more opportunity for snatching up slippery fish. But *Baryonyx* also has long, curved claws, which it uses to hook fish out of the water and into its mouth.

Tail club

T. rex learned long ago to leave *Ankylosaurus* alone. This is a lesson you should learn as well. Sure, *Ankylosaurus* is a calm plant-eater who usually wouldn't hurt a fly. But if something tries to attack, then it will swing its tail wildly, and because the tail ends in a bowling-ball-sized club of bone, it can easily injure anything that it strikes.

Thumb claw

The big plant-eating dinosaur *Iguanodon* looks like a hitchhiker. That's because it has a huge claw on its thumb, which sticks straight out, kind of like how your thumb sticks up when you give a thumbs-up sign. But this claw isn't for show. No, *Iguanodon* uses its claw to defend itself against big meat-eaters.

Bone headed

Pachycephalosaurus has small bumps and horns on much of its head, and the top of its skull is expanded into a big dome of bone. Male *Pachycephalosaurus* fight each other over mates and territory, smashing their skull domes together until one of them falls down.

73

Horned wrestler: *Triceratops*

Triceratops is one of the most famous dinosaurs. You can find it all over the Cretaceous landscape: stampeding in herds across the plains, munching on ferns and bushes in the forests, and even occasionally swimming across rivers!

Bony frill
Triceratops has a big, thin plate of bone sticking out from the back of its head. This is called a frill. The frill anchors jaw muscles and is also a display structure used to attract mates.

Sharp weapons
What does *Triceratops* use its horns for? Many things. *Triceratops* will wrestle each other with their horns for territory, the horns are a fancy display to attract mates, and they are also a great weapon against an attacking *T. rex*!

Three-horned skull
You can spot *Triceratops* from a mile away, because its three-horned skull is so easy to recognize. It has a small horn on its nose, and a long, sharp, curved horn above each eye.

Blade teeth
Triceratops is a champion plant eater. It usually eats over 100 pounds of plants every day! How can it eat so much? It has rows of sharp teeth on each of its jaws. These teeth are closely packed together to form a blade, which cuts and then chews leaves and stems before they are swallowed and digested in the huge gut.

The end of an era

As you've traveled through the age of the dinosaurs, you've seen many fantastic creatures thundering across the land, lurking in the forests, and gliding through the air. You want to continue on this incredible journey, but one day you sense that something's wrong. The sky darkens. Out of nowhere, a huge, deafening crash jolts the earth. As the ground beneath your feet shudders, you know it's time to go home . . . and fast.

What you're witnessing is a six-mile-wide asteroid hitting the planet with the force of millions of bombs. It will cause earthquakes, wildfires, tidal waves, and huge volcanic eruptions. This is not a good time to be alive. Almost every species will die, including *Triceratops*, *T. rex*, and *Velociraptor*. The day of the dinosaurs is at at end. But some lucky animals will survive, able to hide underground away from the chaos. A few of these are small, furry, and warm-blooded.

The day of the mammals is beginning…

Index

To find out more...

NATURAL HISTORY MUSEUM DINO DIRECTORY
An online database featuring each dinosaur's length, diet, and the period when it lived.
http://www.nhm.ac.uk/discover/dino-directory/index.html

WALKING WITH DINOSAURS
See dinosaurs walking the earth with this BBC television series that brings dinosaurs to life through computer graphics.

DINOSAURS by Dr. Steve Brusatte, Quercus, 2008.
A book by Dr. Steve Brusatte with 170 giant-sized, detailed computer-generated images, plus expert text on each species.

DINOSAUR FACTS
Find out facts about different species and even hear clips of how they would have sounded with this website from Dorling Kindersley.
http://www.dkfindout.com/uk/dinosaurs-and-prehistoric-life/dinosaurs/allosaurus

JURASSIC WORLD FIELD GUIDE by Dr. Thomas R. Holtz, Jr. and Dr. Michael Brett-Surman, illustrated by Robert Walters, Random House, 2015.
This non-fiction guide describes over 100 dinosaurs from the Jurassic World film, featuring tons of awesome facts and some of the newest discoveries.

DR. STEVE BRUSATTE is a paleontologist and evolutionary biologist, who specialises in the anatomy and evolution of dinosaurs. He was resident palaeontologist and scientific consultant for the BBC Earth and 20th Century Fox's 2013 film *Walking With Dinosaurs*.

DANIEL CHESTER is co-founder of Moth Collective, an award winning animation and illustration studio. Moth was formed in 2010 to explore a collective passion for all things drawn. www.mothcollective.co.uk

First published in the U.S. in 2016 by
Wide Eyed Editions, an imprint of Quarto Inc.,
The Old Brewery, 6 Blundell Street, London, N7 9BH, UK
QuartoKnows.com
Visit our blogs at QuartoKnows.com

ISBN 978-1-84780-845-5

The artworks were drawn digitally using scanned pencil textures
Set in DIN Alternate, DIN bold, and Mrs Green

Designed by Andrew Watson • Edited by Katie Cotton
Published by Rachel Williams • Production by Jenny Cundill

Manufactured in Dongguan, China TL112017

3 5 7 9 8 6 4